AUSTRALIA

AUSTRALIA

TOM MCKNIGHT
University of California, Los Angeles

THE AMERICAN GEOGRAPHICAL SOCIETY
Around the World Program
HILARY LAMBERT HOPPER
University of Kentucky
Series Editor

The McDonald & Woodward Publishing Company
Blacksburg, Virginia
1996

The McDonald & Woodward Publishing Company
P. O. Box 10308, Blacksburg, Virginia 24062-0308

THE AMERICAN GEOGRAPHICAL SOCIETY
Around the World Program

Australia

© 1995 by The American Geographical Society
The American Geographical Society is the oldest professional geographical society in the United States and a recognized pioneer in geographical research and education.

All rights reserved. First printing, 1996
Composition by Rowan Mountain, Inc., Blacksburg, Virginia
Printed in Canada by Friesen Printers, Altona, Manitoba

02 01 00 99 98 97 96   10 9 8 7 6 5 4 3 2 1

Library of Congress Cataloging-in-Publication Data

McKnight, Tom L. (Tom Lee), 1928–
    Australia, Australia / Tom McKnight.
    p.   cm. — (The American Geographical Society Around the World Program (Series)
    Includes bibliographical references (p.   ).
    ISBN 0-939923-52-1 (lib. : alk. paper). — ISBN 0-939923-51-3 (pbk. : alk. paper)
    1. Australia. I. Title. II. Series: American Geographical Society Around the World Program (Series).
DU96.M34   1996
919.4—dc20   95-48147
                                                                                                                                                     CIP

Cover: The koala is one of the best-known species of Australia's mammals. Beyond its visual appeal that endears it to many humans, the koala symbolizes both the rich and unique biological heritage of Australia and the country's growing appreciation of its natural heritage. Once numbering in the millions and occurring across much of eastern Australia, koalas were nearly driven to extinction by hunting, habitat alteration, and diseases until protective measures were taken during the second half of the twentieth century.

Original sketches by Jennifer Snow. Charts by Rowan Mountain, Inc. Maps by Rowan Mountain, Inc. (p. 54) and Ellen Compton-Gooding (pp. 5, 6, 12, 17, 40, 56).

Photo credits: Australian Department of Foreign Affairs and Trade (Front cover; pp. 13 middle and bottom, 18, 20, 27, 36, 39, 42, 44, 48, 53); Tom McKnight (pp. 13 top, 24, 31, 33, 41, 46).

Mountain High Maps images on p. iv and back cover © 1993 Digital Wisdom, Inc.

Reproduction or translation of any part of this work, except for short excerpts used in reviews, without the written permission of The American Geographical Society is unlawful. Requests for permission to reproduce parts of this work should be addressed to The American Geographical Society, 156 Fifth Avenue, Suite 600, New York, New York 10010.

For additional information about the Around the World Program, please contact the publisher.

———

Dedication

This book is dedicated to the sheilas I have known, especially June Bauer, Berenice Foley, Fay Gale, Beryl Holmes, Vera Mableson, Ann Marshall, Jenny Pigram, and Dot Smith.

Table of Contents

Introduction	1
The Island Continent	4
A European Enclave in Oceania	14
Natural Hazards and Irreverence for the Land	29
Persisting Patterns of Colonial Settlement	34
The Regional Mosaic	40
The Good Luck — Will it Continue?	54
Geographical Milestones in Australian History	58
Sources of Additional Information	59
Australia at a Glance	60

The American Geographical Society

Australia and its place in Oceania.

AUSTRALIA AROUND THE WORLD PROGRAM

THE AMERICAN GEOGRAPHICAL SOCIETY

AUSTRALIA

AUSTRALIA

Australia is the smallest of the world's seven continents and the only one that is encompassed entirely by a single sovereign political unit. With an area of 2,965,368 square miles, Australia is the sixth largest country in the world and is approximately the same size as the forty-eight conterminous states of the United States. It occupies a transitional position between the low and middle latitudes; almost forty percent of its area is within the tropics and the remainder is within the subtropical and temperate parts of the middle latitudes. In general, Australia's physical characteristics are those of a large, relatively compact land mass in the subtropics, although the great extent of aridity and the concentration of population in the least tropical portions of the country tend to de-emphasize human awareness of this subtropical nature. Australia's greatest poleward extent is at the southern end of the island of Tasmania, which reaches beyond 43° south latitude and is roughly as far from the equator as are Boston, Buffalo, and Detroit.

Australia is the most remote of the settled continents. The vast Pacific Ocean washes its eastern and northern shores, the Indian Ocean is to the west, and the frigid waters of the Southern (Antarctic) Ocean are on the south. Australia is some ten thousand miles from Europe, the ancestral home of most of its population. It is six thousand miles from North and South America and four thousand miles from Africa. Only Asia is relatively near, and in the last few years Australia has greatly expanded its contacts and economic relationships with most of the nations of southeastern and southern Asia. Australia's closest diplomatic ties are with the nearby countries of New Zealand and Papua New Guinea.

Although vast in area, Australia is only sparsely populated. Indeed, its population density of six people per square mile is the least of any significant country in the world. Moreover, the population is highly urbanized, with some eighty-five percent living in cities. The population total was about 17,600,000 in 1995, making Australia the forty-third most populous of the world's nations.

Australia is the most arid of the inhabited continents, a fact that is essential to any understanding of its population distribution and agricultural potential. Arable land is limited in extent, and only about one percent of the nation's area is actually planted to crops. Nevertheless, agricultural output could be greatly expanded if there were sufficient markets for the produce.

Politically, the country is divided into six states — New South Wales, Victoria, Queensland, South Australia, Western Australia, and Tasmania — and two territories — Northern Territory and Australian Capital Territory. Each of the states was once a separate British colony; they united to form a single independent nation in 1901. The states vary from big to gigantic in size; indeed, four of the six are larger than Texas. The capital of each state is invariably the dominant urban place of that state, a legacy of colonial days when the administrative center was also the chief port, transportation hub, commercial focus, and principal point of entry for immigrants.

The Largest Cities of Australian States

City	Population (1995)	Percent of State's Population
Sydney, New South Wales	3,600,000	62
Melbourne, Victoria	3,200,000	71
Brisbane, Queensland	1,400,000	43
Perth, Western Australia	1,200,000	71
Adelaide, South Australia	1,100,000	72
Hobart, Tasmania	200,000	40

Other urban places of note are Newcastle, an industrial center of more than 450,000 population in New South Wales; Canberra, the national capital and a rapidly growing city of more than 300,000; Gold Coast, a resort and retirement center of 250,000 on the coast of Queensland; and Wollongong, an industrial city on the south coast of New South Wales.

Australia's flag has a blue ground. The Union Jack in the upper left corner signifies Australia's membership in the Commonwealth of Nations. The five stars of the Southern Cross, four with seven points and one with five points, occupy the right half of the flag. The seven-pointed federal star lies in the lower left quadrant.

THE ISLAND CONTINENT

The Australian environment has unusual characteristics that set it apart from the other continents in a variety of ways.

The fundamental geology of Australia is ancient and stable. In comparison with other continents, it has experienced relatively few major movements of its crust or volcanic activity. It has been subjected to lengthy, relatively uninterrupted periods of weathering and erosion that have reduced its surface to one of low elevation and gentle relief. Spectacular topographic features are rare. Only around the margins, particularly in the east and in a few scattered localities in the interior, are there prominent areas of hills or mountains.

The most notable area of surface irregularity is the Eastern Highlands, a subdued series of mountain ranges that extends the entire length of extreme eastern Australia. In many places, the mountains are so low and subdued that they are almost inconspicuous. Elsewhere there are massive escarpments, sheer cliffs, and deep gorges that almost defy penetration. Nowhere, however, do the mountains reach to impressive elevations; the highest point on the continent, the summit of Mount Kosciusko, is only 7,316 feet above sea level.

West of the Eastern Highlands is a gradual transition from hills to plains, with a continuing decline in elevation; thus the Eastern Highlands merge more or less imperceptibly with the Central Lowlands. The Central Lowlands are broken occasionally by ranges of low, rocky hills, but the dominant characteristics are flat land and level horizons.

A relatively small portion of Australia, located along and near the coast of South Australia, is dominated by a series of parallel broad hills and oceanic gulfs called the Southern Faultlands.

Almost half of the continent consists of an ancient, rigid shield, which has the general appearance of a broad up-

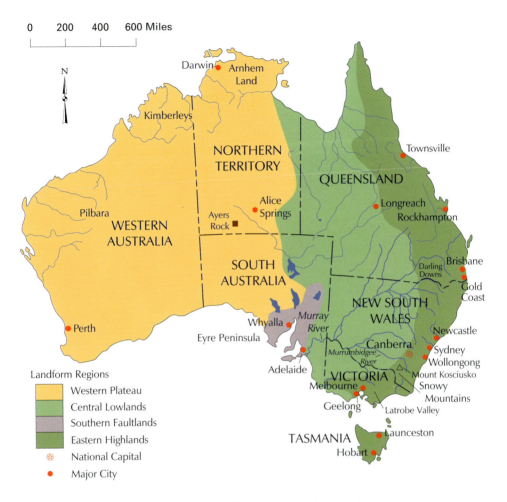

The states and landform regions of Australia.

lifted surface. This is called the Western Plateau. Scattered and isolated mountain ranges interrupt the continuity of the surface of the Western Plateau, but only in three areas has there been general uplift above the plateau — these are the Pilbara country of the far west, the Kimberleys district of the northwest, and Arnhem Land in the far north. Due to the lack of precipitation, most of the Western Plateau is a desert within which are extensive areas covered with many conspicuous long, parallel sand dunes partly stabilized by

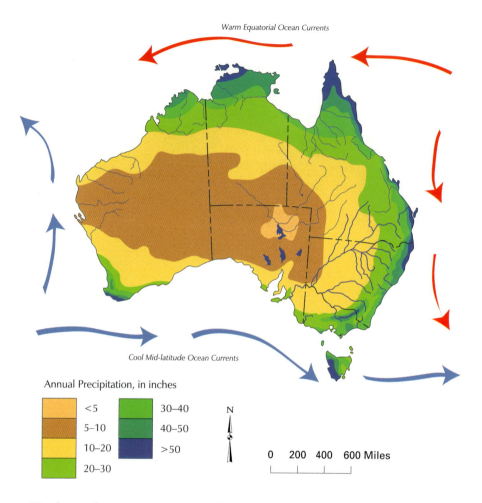

Total annual precipitation in Australia. Precipitation in Australia comes largely from warm, moist tropical air in summer and cooler, moist mid-latitude air in winter. Most precipitation falls as rain near the coast, whereas the vast interior is much drier.

vegetation.

The general lack of diversity among landforms gives rise to broad uniformity of climate, with the result that climatic variation is gradual and transitional over most of the continent. Abrupt changes of climate are few.

Even so, the dominant trait of the Australian climate — its aridity — is in great part the result of the position of the Eastern Highlands relative to the moisture-bearing winds blowing toward the continent. Although this cordillera is neither high nor broad, its north-south orientation intercepts the prevailing easterly winds, thus preventing the moist Pacific air masses from reaching the greater part of the continent. This is by no means the only cause of Australia's widespread aridity but it is a major one.

About half of the continent is a desert, and another fourth is semi-desert. These dry lands occupy all of the interior and much of the western part of Australia. This is a subtropical desert, with summers that are scorchingly hot and whose unpleasantness is emphasized by gusty winds, blowing sand, and persistent bushflies. Winter, on the other hand, is characterized by long stretches of pleasant weather, with clear skies, bright sunshine, and mild temperatures which may become quite chilly at night.

Only a small proportion of the Australian population lives in the dry region. Human settlement is mostly in the eastern and southeastern coastal zones, areas which have relatively abundant rainfall that is well distributed seasonally and reasonably dependable from year to year.

There are two areas with particularly distinctive climates — the far north and the southwestern corners of the continent. The climate of Australia's far north is dominated by the seasonal reversals of the monsoon. During three to five months of summer, persistent northerly oceanic winds bring abundant moisture, thunderstorms, and tropical storms. For the remainder of the year, high pressure develops over the land and outblowing southerly airflow more or less completely inhibits precipitation on land. The southwestern "corners" of the continent — areas centering on Perth in Western Australia and Adelaide in South Australia — have a distinctive "Mediterranean" climate where winter is the wet season and summer is almost rainless.

Australia — because of its climate and topographic characteristics — has the smallest supply of surface water and the most remarkable conditions of underground water of any of the settled continents. With very restricted areas of abundant rainfall, it is logical to expect that surface streams are few and small. Indeed, nearly three-quarters of

The Great Barrier Reef

Off the northeastern coast of Australia is the Great Barrier Reef, the longest and largest living coral formation in the world. Despite its name, this is not a single extensive reef; rather, it is a chain of more than 2,500 individual reefs that vary in size from isolated pinnacles to massive structures up to fifteen miles long and fifty square miles in area. Some three-hundred-twenty coral islands, nearly all of them quite small, are interspersed among the reefs. This enormous "reef province," as scientists prefer to call it, trends generally north-south for twelve hundred miles, spans about 15° of latitude, and extends over some ninety thousand square miles of ocean. At some points it is only a few miles from the mainland; at others, it is almost two hundred miles offshore.

A coral reef is formed when tiny animals called coral polyps attach themselves to the shallow sea bottom and secrete limy external skeletons around the lower half of their bodies. These tiny creatures, most only a fraction of an inch long, live in colonies of countless individuals, attaching themselves to one another both with living tissue and their external skeletons. Their extraordinary abundance is a tribute to their remarkable reproductive capabilities, because they are not actually very hardy creatures. They cannot survive in water that is very cool or very fresh or very dirty. Moreover, they require considerable light, so they cannot live more than a few tens of feet below the surface of the ocean.

Under the best of circumstances, a coral colony cannot build a reef unaided. The many openings in and among the skeletons must be filled in and cemented together by other processes. Much of the infilling material consists of fine sediment that is provided by other marine animals through their borings and waste

---

the continent is largely without permanent streamflow, and Australia's largest river — the Murray — carries only four percent as much water as does the Mississippi River.

In contrast to the scarce surface water, Australia's underground water resources are unusually plentiful. The continent contains extensive artesian basins underlying much of the interior. Unfortunately, however, most of this underground water is too salty for either human consumption or use in irrigation, although much of it can be used by livestock.

The plant and animal life of Australia is remarkably distinctive, evolution having followed paths that were not followed on any other continent. Most significant to the geographic landscape is the unusual natural vegetation. Dense forest is scarce, and nearly all of

products, and a host of tiny animals and plants contribute their skeletons and shells when they die. Indispensable to the reef-forming process are cement and mortar provided by algae and other tiny forms of "seaweed."

As with most reefs, the Great Barrier Reef formed on a slowly sinking seabed. As sinking progressed, the deeper corals died and their skeletons provided a firm foundation upon which more polyps secreted more skeletons in the shallower "live" portion of the reef. Near the surface, the reef-building flattens and expands horizontally. The resultant "barrier" interrupts wave action and water circulation, creating different environments on each side of the reef. The protected inner (shoreward) side is bathed in warmer, placid waters, whereas the outer side receives the full force of the pounding sea.

Although corals are the dominant creatures of the reef, a great variety of other animals and plants shares the habitat, making a coral reef one of the richest ecosystems known. Mollusks, such as clams, cowries, cones, snails, sea slugs, squids, and octopuses, are particularly common. Also notable are such crustaceans as shrimp, crabs, lobsters, and crayfish, and echinoderms such as starfish and sand dollars. Fishes occupy the reef environment in enormous numbers and variety. Other common vertebrates include sea turtles, sea snakes, dolphins, and whales. And, the small coral islands are home to vast numbers of sea birds.

Most of the Great Barrier Reef has been set aside by the Australian government as a national maritime park and is recognized by the International Union for the Conservation of Nature as a World Heritage Site. The reef is one of Australia's most compelling tourist attractions, for both domestic and international visitors.

the continent is vegetated with grassland, shrubland, or relatively open woodland. At the other extreme, however, the arid desert regions are clothed in a surprising amount of vegetation. In all but the very driest areas there tends to be a plant cover of high shrubs or low trees that seems to belie the sparse rainfall.

The major plant associations are distributed somewhat like concentric rings outward from the arid interior. A narrow forest zone, including disconnected patches of rainforest, occurs along the east coast, in Tasmania, and in the far southwest. Inland from the forest, and encircling most of the continent, is a zone of eucalyptus woodland, mostly quite open. Further inland is an incomplete ring of mixed grassland and shrubland. In the core of the continent but displaced toward the west, is an

Exotic Wildlife

In addition to native forms of wildlife, non-native — or exotic — species are conspicuous elements in the present fauna of Australia. These exotics have been introduced to the continent by accident or design, and have become established in the wild. Two factors account for the significance of non-native species in the Australian fauna: (1) native animals are generally limited, specialized, unaggressive, and vulnerable, making it relatively easy for an exotic to become established, once it is introduced, and (2) European settlers, particularly in the nineteenth century, were often eager to introduce animals from the "old country" to "improve" upon the sparse and unusual native fauna of Australia.

The earliest of the exotic introductions was the dingo, which apparently was brought to Australia by Aboriginal migrants from Southeast Asia, and has been a well-established member of the fauna for many centuries. The most notable recent introduction is the European rabbit, whose spread from an initial release of twenty-four animals near Melbourne in 1859 to a half-continent plague within fifty years is the classic scare story of all mammalian importations. The diffusion of the European fox over Australia was even more expansive — the rabbit never moved into the northern third of the continent, whereas the fox has spread to every corner of the land.

In many ways the proliferation of feral livestock in Australia is even more spectacular than the story of either the rabbit or the fox. One of the most striking discrepancies between Australian wildlife and that of other continents is the total lack of native ungulates, or hoofed animals, in Australia. Ungulates are generally large, gregarious, and widespread; thus their presence is normally conspicuous in the landscape, and their absence from Australia is a notable zoogeographical oddity.

All six of the common mid-latitude barnyard animals — horses, donkeys,

extensive area that is largely desert; its flora is varied, but is dominated by expansive areas of massive "hummock" grasses, mostly species of spinifex.

If Australia's flora is unusual, its fauna is absolutely bizarre. Its assemblage of terrestrial animal life is without parallel in other parts of the world, and even its bird life is significantly different from that of other continents. As the tectonic plates of Gondwanaland separated and moved apart, the Australian plate became cut off from most of the rest of the world. This isolation, over millions of years, nurtured the evolution of strange, sometimes rare, and vulnerable species. Placental mammals, the dominant animals of other

cattle, sheep, goats, and pigs — have been bred as domesticated livestock in considerable numbers over most of the settled parts of Australia. In addition, two more specialized varieties of subtropical livestock — camels and water buffaloes — were brought to Australia in limited numbers. All of these species, except sheep, on occasion have escaped from confinement or deliberately been turned loose and have established sizeable free-ranging populations in various parts of the country, thus becoming *feral* in the true sense of the term.

At present, Australia has more feral horses, donkeys, cattle, goats, water buffaloes, and camels than any other country in the world, and ranks second to the United States in the number of feral pigs. The total number of feral animals in the country varies from year to year, but is in the general vicinity of four million individuals. There are also uncountable numbers of feral dogs and cats.

The presence of such a vast population of exotic wildlife is almost universally deplored. Most objections are on economic grounds, particularly by pastoralists. Dingoes are effective predators on sheep; rabbits and feral ungulates inhibit pastoral operations, primarily by consuming feed and water that graziers want for their livestock, but also by a variety of other transgressions; foxes, feral dogs, and feral cats devastate such native wildlife as ground-nesting birds, lizards, and vulnerable marsupials.

Consequently, enormous efforts have been, and continue to be, expended to control these exotics by such measures as poisoning, trapping, shooting, and building barrier fences. The implacable opposition of the pastoral industry to these animals is thoroughly understandable from an economic point of view. And even when considered from the loftier ethic of the integrity of the continental ecosystem, it would seem the better part of wisdom to beware of the persistence of such exotic animals in the wild. One of the broad lessons of history is that humankind's tampering with the biota usually has unsatisfactory results.

continents, are few and inconspicuous in Australia. The characteristic mammals of Australia are the relatively primitive marsupials, animals that give birth to partially formed, almost embryonic, young that develop after birth for a long period in the mother's pouch. The dominance of marsupials in the Australian fauna is represented by the variety of species that have evolved and the diversity of ecological niches that they have filled.

As the global center of surviving primitive mammals, Australia is also the home of the world's only living monotremes, the egg-laying duck-bill platypus and the spiny anteater.

THE AMERICAN GEOGRAPHICAL SOCIETY

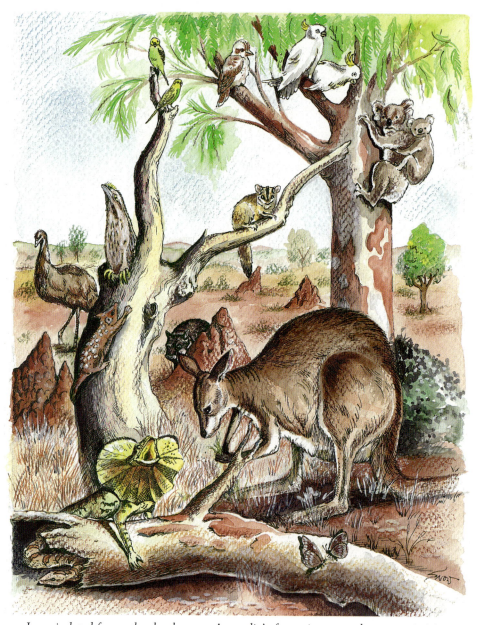

Long isolated from other land areas, Australia's fauna is among the most primitive and bizarre on earth. Here, set in an open eucalypt woodland, can be seen crow butterflies, death adder, frilled lizard, budgerigars, cockatoos, emu, tawny frogmouth, kookaburra, koalas, sugar glider, native cat, kangaroo, and wombat.

AUSTRALIA AROUND THE WORLD PROGRAM

THE AMERICAN GEOGRAPHICAL SOCIETY

Baobab trees, with thick trunks and few branches, occur in the western Monsoonal North of Australia.

Lush rain forest, found in parts of northern and eastern Australia, is an exception to the continent's generally dry-land forms of vegetation.

Aborigines assemble near Ayers Rock, or Uluru, in Australia's Northern Territory. Aboriginal culture traditionally considers Uluru to be the mother of the earth.

AROUND THE WORLD PROGRAM **AUSTRALIA**

A European Enclave

IN OCEANIA

Australia's recorded history is quiet and relatively uneventful, except for the long and relentless process whereby the Aboriginal inhabitants were dispossessed by European settlers, mostly in the nineteenth century. Apart from this typical colonial experience, there were no invasions, no civil wars, no revolutions, not even any formidable opposition from the natives. Australia is a nation that grew in relatively tame and orderly fashion from its first convict settlement to federation in little more than a century.

The unique and remote Australian environment provided a home for a distinctive society of people known simply as Australian Aborigines. This society, with its Paleolithic culture, was well adjusted to the harsh realities of life on an arid continent. The first Aboriginal migrants came to Australia from the general area of the East Indies at least 40,000 years ago. It is worth noting that the written history of European Australia encompasses perhaps seven generations, but the Aboriginal prehistory of the continent comprises at least two thousand generations!

The remarkable Aborigines were relatively few in number (considering the vast area of the continent), racially separate from the rest of the world, naked hunters and gatherers that were houseless, artistic, mystical, and enclosed within firm and intricate social patterns. Thus, they were essentially Stone Age people fitted to survive in a fierce and generally unproductive habitat as long as there was no significant competition with more complex societies.

After thousands of years of isolation, however, the Aborigines were confronted abruptly with alien invaders whose arrival signaled the conclusion of a way of life as surely as if extraterrestrial beings had landed on Earth. The most technologically advanced nation in the world (the steam engine had just been invented in Britain) came face to face with a host of some of the world's most primitive mini-tribes.

From a prehistoric total of perhaps three-hundred thousand Aborigines and no Europeans, the population of Australia has grown to more than seventeen million, less than two percent of whom contain Aboriginal blood. The present population mix, then, is essentially the result of long-continued primarily-European immigration, the pattern of which has fluctuated significantly through the years.

The major characteristics of the Australian population are generally similar to those of other industrialized, or developed, nations, with a few notable exceptions. It is unusual that such a large country should have such a small population, but the environmental and historical reasons for this circumstance are clear.

In terms of immigration, Australia has been one of the leading recipient countries of the world throughout most of its recorded history. It has been a prominent destination of European emigrants for many decades. The ma-

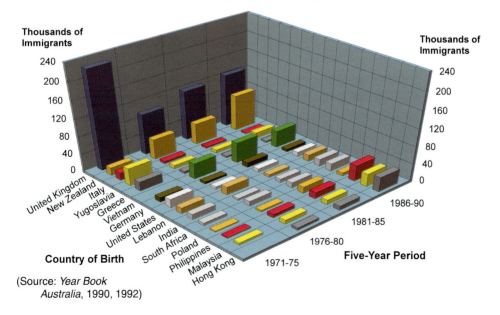

Birthplace of Settlers Arriving in Australia
Fifteen Leading Countries of Origin

(Source: *Year Book Australia*, 1990, 1992)

jority of all immigrants came from the British Isles until after World War II, at which time more continental Europeans started coming to Australia. The largest numbers of non-British migrants since World War II have been Italians, followed by Greeks, Dutch, Yugoslavs, Germans, and Poles. Within the last decade or so there has been a significant increase in immigration from Asia, particularly from Vietnam, the Phillipines, Malaysia, and Hong Kong.

The net increase in Australia's population from immigration since 1975 has been about ninety thousand per year, amounting to some thirty-five percent of the total population increase in that period.

The current population of Australia, then, is ethnically varied, but the ethnic groups are largely of European origin. People of British origin are still dominant and make up more than one-third of the total population. Continental Europeans are broadly represented, with only a few exceptions — most notably people of French origin. A small but rapidly expanding component of Asians is present. The Aboriginal component of the population is also growing rapidly; census totals are incomplete, but the number of Aborigines in Australia today probably exceeds four-hundred thousand.

The general pattern of population distribution strongly reflects environmental, particularly climatic, influences. The drier parts of the continent are less suitable than the wetter parts for farming and livestock raising and, as a result, are sparsely populated. The humid areas, particularly the mid-lati-

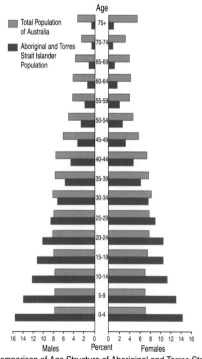

Comparison of Age Structure of Aboriginal and Torres Strait Islander Population and Total Population, 1991 Census.
Source: 1991 Census of Population and Housing; Adapted from *Year Book of Australia 1992*.

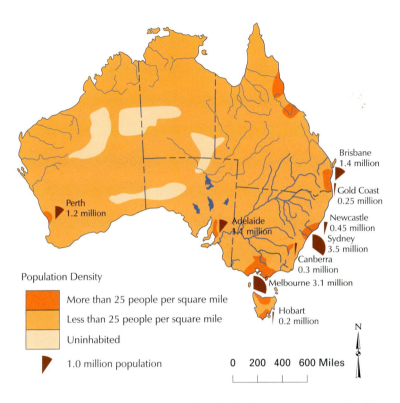

Australia is the least-densely populated of the inhabited continents. Nearly all important urban areas are located on the coast, especially the southeastern and southwestern coasts.

tude portions, permit more fruitful use of the land and are occupied in moderate density. The only areas of high density settlement are urban or urban-related. Thus, the major concentration of people tends to be in an arc of moderately dense population extending around the southeastern coast from Rockhampton in Queensland to Whyalla in South Australia. Major urban centers punctuate this crescent as nodes of high density, but there are also areas of sparse settlement, such as the Australian Alps in New South Wales and Victoria. Beyond the arc, moderate population density occurs in the southeastern and northern coastal portions of Tasmania, in the southwest of Western Australia, and in various valleys of the east coast of Queensland. Most of the remainder of the continent, some eighty percent of its area, is

The American Geographical Society

Sydney, capital of New South Wales, is Australia's largest city. Prominent landmarks recognized throughout the world include the Sydney Opera House and Harbor Bridge.

very thinly populated, with large desert areas in Western Australia and Northern Territory essentially devoid of any human inhabitants.

Perhaps the most striking feature of Australian demography is the extreme concentration of its population; some sixty-two percent of the total population resides in the seven capital cities. In contrast, the seven largest metropolitan areas in the United States contain only sixteen percent of the population; comparable statistics are nineteen percent for Great Britain, twenty-three percent for France, and thirty-five percent for Canada. Another twenty-four percent of Australia's people lives in smaller urban areas, and only fourteen percent can be classed as rural. Such metropolitan centralization has been a long-established characteristic, as an historic holdover from the days of separate colonies. Only in the 1980s, for the first time, did a slight trend of movement to smaller centers and rural areas set in.

With the notable exception of the Aborigines, Australian culture is a clear reflection of its northwest European heritage. There have been various original contributions, but contemporary Australian society owes its basic structure to its British and, to a lesser extent, continental European roots. This is shown in most facets of life, from governmental structure to cuisine to art forms to sports. Nonetheless, a distinctive Australian imprint is often discernable, particularly in adjustments to the climatic differences between Australia and Britain, such as emphasis on beach-oriented and other outdoor activities and tropical architectural styles. Moreover, Aboriginal art forms, and in some cases music, have flourished as parallel developments that are only recently beginning to be melded into the popular culture.

Australians are for the most part at least nominally Christian. The principal denominations are Anglican, Roman Catholic, and Uniting Church, the latter a combination of Methodists, Congregationalists, and Presbyterians. Non-Christian religious affiliation has been growing in recent years in direct relation to immigration from Asian countries, but the total is still small. In point of fact, most Australians do not attend religious observances with much frequency or regularity.

Australia is overwhelmingly a monolingual country, with the Aussie version of English spoken and understood everywhere. Other languages are significant in only two settings. At the time of European contact there were some three hundred Aboriginal languages extant. All but about two dozen of these have become either extinct or inconspicuous. However, wherever there is a concentration of Aborigines today, there is likely to be an almost exclusive use of one or more of the surviving Aboriginal languages. Various European or Asian languages are of some importance in urban ethnic neighborhoods. Most widely used are Italian, Greek, and several Slavic languages.

The egalitarian nature of Australian society is a matter of both pride and dispute. The concept of "mateship" is ingrained in Australian folklore as the hallmark of a classless society, presumably as an outgrowth of the convict forebears of the present populace. This does not mean that prejudice and discrimination are absent, but it seems clear that Australian society has less factionalism than is present in many other countries.

One further aspect of culture that deserves mention in this brief summary is the Aussie love of sport, both as participant and as spectator. Most of the

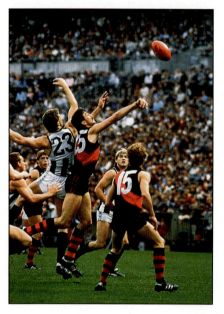

The Australian rules football grand final in Melbourne regularly draws more than 100,000 spectators.

Love of Sport

More than one million girls and women participate annually in organized sport in Australia.

population lives near the ocean, and the combination of warm weather and magnificent beaches beckons during much of the year. The result is a heavy use of sand and surf by a sunbronzed populace. Organized sports are also widespread and popular. Cricket dominates the summer scene, away from the beaches. Winter is football time, and in Australia that means four different forms of the game: Aussie rules football, rugby league, rugby union, and soccer. Basketball has been growing rapidly in favor, and tennis and golf have an enduring popularity. Perhaps the most popular sport of all, however, is horse racing, which is also a focal point of another facet of the Australian character — the love of gambling.

Several social issues are important in contemporary Australia, and the following are among the more important.

Monarchy versus Republicanism. Although Australia has been an independent country since 1901, it has maintained formal allegiance to Great Britain in several ways, most notably by recognizing the British monarch as the official head of state for Australia. In recent years sentiment has been rising to dissolve all official ties with the monarchy, although a sizable part of the population is militantly in favor of retaining the *status quo*. It is likely that this proposition will be brought to a popular vote in Australia in the near future.

Development versus preservation. Throughout most of its history, relatively little attention has been paid to conservation and preservation of natural resources in Australia. Only in the last quarter century has conservation consciousness blossomed. Today, ecological concerns and sustainable development concepts have become widely, but by no means universally, accepted in the national political, social, and economic agenda.

Aboriginal concerns. Although representing only a tiny portion of the population, Aborigines obviously occupy a special place in Australian society. Long underprivileged, undereducated, underemployed, and often unnoticed, their presence is increasingly manifest as their financial and political power grows. Vocal demands for "land rights" are being addressed by politicians and judges, and the 1992 Mabo

A Young Man's Decision

Peter Hanrick was deep in thought. He paid no attention to the familiar surroundings through which his horse slowly picked its way. The blazing sun of late October, the whine of the persistent bushflies, the depressing sight of dusty plain where waving Mitchell grassland should be — none of these penetrated Peter's conscious thought. He had a decision to make, and soon. It should have been resolved months ago, but he just hadn't been able to make up his mind.

Peter had lived on "Talleyrand" station all his life; in fact he represented the third generation of Hanricks on this property. Although they didn't actually own the land, they had a long-term lease that gave them considerable security of tenure. It was the only home Peter had ever known. He loved the freedom of the open spaces and the close-to-nature lifestyle of the extensive sheep raiser. Yet he was also attracted by the lure of the world beyond the horizon. He yearned, somewhat, to experience life in the city, and perhaps to travel much more widely.

The Talleyrand homestead is situated thirty-two miles, mostly over dirt roads, from Longreach, in central Queensland. Longreach is a reasonably typical Outback town, although a bit larger and more prosperous than most. With six thousand residents, it is the largest town for four-hundred-fifty miles in any direction. The country round about is normally some of the best pasture land in interior Australia; in good years there are about a million sheep and one-third that many beef cattle within one hundred miles of Longreach. But this has not been a good year; nor have the three preceding it. Central Queensland is suffering from a four-year drought; the normal annual rainfall in Longreach is sixteen inches, but in the last four years the *total* has been sixteen inches! So the landscape is dry, dusty, and de-grassed, and most graziers have had to reduce their flocks and herds by fifty percent or more.

Peter had completed high school ten months ago, receiving his Senior Certificate from Longreach Secondary School. He had made high marks in school, and would have been eligible to attend university, but he was not sure that was what he wanted to do, so he had stayed at Talleyrand and worked full-time for his father as a jackeroo. It was now imperative, however, that he submit his application to university if he planned to attend. His alternative plan was to attend Stockmen's College, a unique technical training institute located in Longreach. With an enrollment of about fifty-five students, it provides practical and technical training in the art of raising sheep and cattle, in a two-year course.

This was Peter's dilemma: to apply to the University of Queensland in Brisbane, twelve hundred miles away, or to enroll at Stockmen's College in Longreach. The latter would be safe and familiar; he knew the town and its environs well, and most of the people were friends or acquaintances. His parents were pillars of the community; his father supported various community causes and was a tireless worker in the ongoing efforts to establish a museum — The Pastoral and Outback Hall of Fame — on the outskirts of town. His mother was very active in the Countrywomen's Association and was known throughout central Queensland for her knitting and other handicraft work. If Peter stayed in Longreach, he would be with his old friends, continue a familiar lifestyle, and begin dropping in to one of the four local pubs at beer time. The annual rodeo and gymkhana would still be the highlight of his year.

If he went to the university, his life would change markedly. He was not a stranger to Brisbane, as he visited there with his family and had spent a memorable four days there with some of his mates after graduation last year. But this would mean living on campus in a residential college — probably Scots College, run by the Anglican Church — participating in extracurricular activities, seeing major rugby matches and national and even international cricket tests, going to the beach with some frequency "just like a normal Aussie," being exposed to new cultural and recreational opportunities, and probably becoming a heavy beer drinker somewhat earlier in life.

All of these thoughts turned in Peter's mind as his horse took him across the southeastern quarter of Talleyrand's forty thousand acres. Suddenly he came back to reality as a four-foot-long sand goanna, a monitor lizard, burst from a clump of gidgee scrub. He guided his horse toward Big Billabong, a waterhole in the otherwise-dry bed of the Thomson River that crossed the property. Even in severe droughts, Big Billabong retained some water. The westering sun sent reflections across the billabong, as well as shadows of the big coolibah and red gum trees that lined its edges. There were ducks swimming in the water, cockatoos screeching in the trees, and a kookaburra laughing in the distance. Two startled wallabies bounded away. Several dozen sheep on the other side of the pond skittishly moved into the scrub as Peter approached.

Peter felt a sudden glow of pride when he thought of the sheep. His father was one of the most careful of pastoralists, and, unlike most of his neighbors, did not overstock his land. In the good years he grazed twelve thousand Merinos on Talleyrand, although it would support twice that number. And in the bad years he could also carry twelve thousand, as overgrazing and overbrowsing had not decimated the forage before the dry times came.

As the sun dropped below the horizontal horizon, Peter turned his horse back toward the homestead. The harshness of the environment was lost on him. He saw only its beauty, its familiarity, its satisfaction. If he were to make his final decision at that moment, the university wouldn't stand a chance. But in the clear light of tomorrow, who knows?

decision brought Aboriginal interests to the forefront of public debate as never before when the Australian High Court affirmed for the first time that Aborigines had rights to common law land title under certain circumstances. The limitations of this judgment are not totally clear, and it has resulted in widespread uncertainty in many aspects of Australian economic, social, and political life.

The Gender Gap. Although women were allowed to vote and to run for political office very early in Australian history, Australia has long been a bastion of male privilege. In recent years, however, women have assumed a much higher profile in political and economic affairs. 1992 was "The Year of the Woman" in Australia, and its unofficial maxim — "Some leaders are born women" — is now recognized as more than just a clever phrase.

Australia is a country of the "developed" world, with a mixed but generally well-endowed array of resources, a small population, a well-established transportation and communication infrastructure, a substantial manufacturing sector, an urban-oriented society, a capitalistic economic system, and a remote location *vis-a-vis* most other developed countries.

The phrase "Australia rides the sheep's back" is one of the enduring generalizations of Australian history. The early European settlers soon discovered the twin handicaps of making a living off the land in Australia — environmental problems, particularly as

Merino sheep water at a seasonally-transient pond near Wangaratta in Victoria.

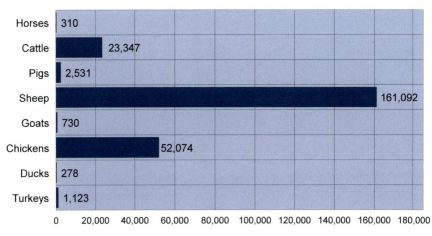

(Source: *The Far East and Australia*, Europa Publications, 1994)

regards water and soil, and economic problems, particularly in terms of distance to markets. There was, however, a lot of grass in Australia, and wool was a non-perishable product that could withstand a long, slow trip to distant markets. Consequently, various breeds of sheep were introduced to Australia, and it was soon recognized that the Merino breed was particularly well suited to local conditions, as it was both hardy and an excellent wool producer.

Before long an Australian strain of Merino was developed, and sheep raising was tried in every part of the continent except the driest deserts. There were many failures, and some areas, primarily in the tropical portions of the country, were never suitable for sheep. In general, however, sheep found a happy home in the austral continent, and sheep raising continues to be by far the most widespread form of land use. There are still nine times more sheep than people in Australia.

The early development of a cattle industry was not as widespread as that of sheep. Generally, beef cattle raising has taken place in areas not suitable for sheep raising or dairying, although beef cattle are associated with both in more moist areas. In recent years, there has been a significant increase in beef husbandry, with the number of animals almost doubling in the last decade.

Dairying is a major rural industry, pig and poultry raising are more limited, and a notable recent development is the raising of goats.

Australia is almost self-sufficient in agricultural produce. The only farm products that must be imported in quantity are such tropical specialties as tea, coffee, and chocolate. Moreover, agricultural exports have long been significant to the national economy.

Farming occupies only a small fraction of the continent, partly because the proper combination of climate, terrain, and soils is limited and partly because export markets are often restricted and distant. The major agricultural zone, within which farming occurs in discontinuous segments, extends around the southeastern edge of the country in the form of a crescent that is one hundred to two-hundred-fifty miles wide, with its northeastern extremity in the Darling Downs of southeastern Queensland and its western end on the Eyre Peninsula of South Australia.

There is a comparably placed, although smaller, band in the southwestern part of Western Australia. Other significant but much smaller farming areas are in the coastal valleys of Queensland and Tasmania and along some of the inland rivers in southeastern Australia.

Wheat, by far the most important crop, occupies about half the tilled acreage in Australia. Other important grains include barley, oats, rice, grain sorghums, and corn. Sugar cane is the leading specialty crop; it is grown intensively on patches of fertile lowland along the coast of Queensland and northernmost New South Wales. Other prominent crops in Australia include grapes, citrus fruit, a wide range of deciduous fruit, bananas, vegetables, potatoes, cotton, tobacco, and various oilseeds.

The extraction and processing of minerals has been a major facet of the economic development of Australia, almost from the time of earliest European settlement. A wide variety of these resources is found in commercial quantities, giving the country an important base for industrialization. In recent years, Australia has become one of the world's leading mineral exporters. Furthermore, the establishment of mining centers, often in remote localities, has boosted the spread of settlement, and some of the mineral discoveries have sharply stimulated immigration to Australia.

Coal and iron ore are the twin keystones of the mining industry. They are sufficiently abundant to provide for all domestic needs and make Australia one of the world's leading exporters of both. The country also has major supplies of several important metals and ranks among the half-dozen leading producers of lead, zinc, silver, bauxite, and nickel. Other important minerals include gold, copper, manganese, and precious stones. The country must import some petroleum, but continuing exploration has discovered significant oil and gas resources in widely scattered areas.

The Australian economy has all the characteristics of a modern, industrialized nation. Manufacturing developed under several handicaps, but has become well established. The industrial structure of Australia is diversified, reflecting the fact that Australian manufacturers supply most of the wide range of goods required by the domestic consumer market. The principal types of manufacturing are transportation equipment (especially automobiles), food processing, and machinery production.

Most Australian factories are located in the major metropolitan areas. More than ninety percent of all manufactur-

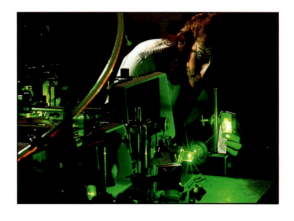

As Australia's economy matures, its manufacturing and service industries are becoming technologically competitive with the rest of the world.

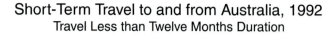

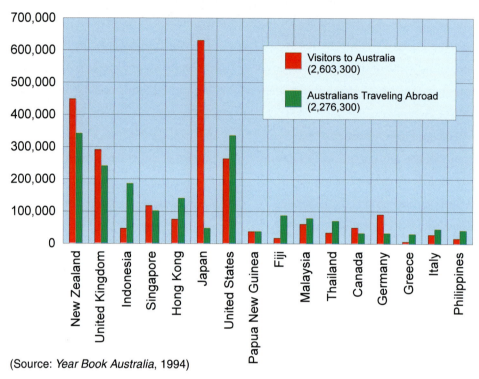

(Source: *Year Book Australia*, 1994)

Tourism is becoming an increasingly important element in the Australian economy.

ing is found within the crescent-shaped coastal zone between Rockhampton, Queensland, and Whyalla, South Australia, and the vast majority is concentrated between Newcastle, New South Wales, and Geelong, Victoria. Indeed, manufacturing is even more concentrated in the principal cities than population is. In the five mainland states, the proportion of manufacturing located in the capitals ranges from a high of eighty-six percent in Melbourne to a low of sixty-six percent in Brisbane. Sydney and Melbourne are the largest industrial centers, containing between them nearly three-fifths of the nation's factories.

NATURAL HAZARDS

AND IRREVERENCE FOR THE LAND

Although most Australians live in cities and are insulated from the vagaries of Nature, the national economy and social well-being are nonetheless dependent on the country's environment. The rural industries of crop growing and livestock raising have always been bulwarks of the economy. Rural Australians, and sometimes their urban counterparts, are afflicted from time to time by four notable natural hazards — droughts, floods, cyclones, and bushfires.

Australia is a country that is half desert and one-fourth semi-desert. Arid regions receive precipitation that is not only scarce but also unreliable; there is often wide fluctuation from the average in any given year. An arid continent like Australia can expect to experience below-normal rainfall with considerable frequency. Indeed, drought is a recurrent phenomenon in many parts of the country, and it is not unusual for large areas to endure five or ten consecutive years of drought.

Although the native Australian plant and animal life is adapted to aridity, and the most prominent breeds of sheep (Merino) and beef cattle (Hereford and Shorthorn) can survive conditions of considerable harshness, any prolonged drought brings severe hardship to rural Australians. Many head of livestock literally starve to death, and many others must be slaughtered prematurely to reduce the herd sizes to fit the diminished forage. It is little wonder that drought is the primary concern of most Australian pastoralists.

Farmers, too, can be seriously affected by drought. The major grains (wheat, barley, oats), in particular, experience dwindling yields in dry times. Irrigation has become increasingly widespread in Australia, in part to serve as a buffer against drought. Water storage and distribution projects are widely used by farmers in the watershed of the Murray River and, to a lesser extent, in many other drainage basins.

One of the major ironies of the Australian environment is the fact that flooding is also a significant natural hazard on this the driest of the inhabited continents. Most flood problems result from intense localized rainstorms along the humid east coast of the country, where narrow valleys and flat floodplains are vulnerable to concentrated runoff. In addition, much of the Monsoonal North experiences annual flooding during the heavy summer rains. And even in the arid interior there are occasional episodes of flooding that are particularly stressful because of their unexpectedness.

Various kinds of storms affect Australia, but by far the most devastating are tropical cyclones, identical to hurricanes in the United States. These intense low pressure systems strike the northeastern (Queensland), northern (Northern Territory), and northwestern (Western Australia) coasts from three to six times a year, always in the Southern Hemisphere summer. Their mighty winds and tempestuous rains can do immense damage to coastal areas. For example, a cyclone hit Darwin, the administrative center for the Northern Territory, on Christmas morning, 1974, killing sixty people and destroying or damaging almost every building in the urban area.

It should be noted, however, that destruction and tragedy are not the only legacy of cyclones. Rainfall associated with cyclones is often a critical source of moisture for the parched Outback. Although devastation may result in the immediate path of the storm, a much more extensive area may be nurtured by the life-giving rains.

Two characteristics of the environment — vegetation that is eminently flammable, and the widespread extent of dry conditions — make Australia particularly susceptible to wildfires. As a result, wildfires — invariably referred to as "bushfires" in Australia — are to be anticipated with considerable frequency over much of the continent. The Monsoonal North is especially prone to burning; during the long dry season bushfire smoke is almost constantly on the horizon. Even the arid portions of the Outback, with sparse but flammable vegetation, experience frequent fires. The more densely vegetated regions — the forests and woodlands of the east and southeast — also are susceptible to fire, particularly during periods of drought.

Bushfires may cause devastation and hardship on the local flora and fauna, as well as on crops, pastures, and livestock. Moreover, in some cases out-of-control fires, usually intensified by drought and high winds, sweep through settlements, leaving death and destruction in their wake. For example, the infamous "Ash Wednesday" fires of February, 1983, caused seventy-one human deaths and hundreds of millions of dollars worth of property damage in Victoria and South Australia.

It should be noted, however, that a bushfire is a catastrophic event but does not necessarily create long-term damage. Many plants regenerate better after fires, and the ecosystem is often healthier in the long run for experiencing fairly frequent burning.

The pattern of resource exploitation and land utilization in Australia has been one of short-term considerations, with little thought to future consequences. This is a common occurrence when a relatively small number of immigrants invade a new and unspoiled continent; it has been characteristic of frontier settlements throughout human history. In many ways Australia is still a frontier country. The population is relatively small and the land to be "conquered" is vast. Although frontier attitudes toward the land still prevail, twentieth century technology is brought to bear. The bulldozer becomes the deity and the cloud of dust becomes the symbol of contemporary Australian civilization. "Development"

A brushfire burns in Kakadu National Park, Northern Territory, during the dry season.

of the land is important, but development based upon exploitation without conservation is rapacious. The sorry spectacle of nineteenth century resource depletion in North America has been and is being repeated in Australia. In spite of the prominence of rural industries in Australian consciousness, there has been little reverence for the land.

Until very recently, a positive approach to the land resource was apparent only in three general endeavors — impounding surface waters, tapping

The Snowy Mountains Scheme

Australia is the locale of one of the world's most ambitious water storage and diversion enterprises, the Snowy Mountains Scheme. This scheme is a dual purpose project that was begun in 1949 to generate hydroelectricity and provide water for irrigation. Construction required a quarter of a century and was substantially completed in 1974. The general plan was a simple one, but its implementation was difficult and expensive.

The eastern slopes of the Snowy Mountains in southern New South Wales, the highest part of the Eastern Highlands, receive considerable precipitation year-round. The rivers that drain this area southeasterly into the Pacific Ocean carry a great deal of water that is unused by people and thus flows into the sea as a "wasted" resource. The heart of the Snowy Mountains Scheme is the impounding of two of these rivers — the Snowy and the Eucumbene — and diverting much of their flow through trans-mountain tunnels to the west slope of the range. This water is used to generate hydroelectricity and is then added to the Murray and Murrumbidgee rivers, where most of it is used for irrigation projects downstream.

Major construction included seventeen large dams and many small ones, nine power stations, about one hundred miles of tunnels, eighty miles of aqueducts, and many miles of high-voltage electricity transmission lines. The enormous cost of the scheme has been roughly one billion dollars, but its results are impressive. The average annual electricity output is more than five billion kWh, and the average annual addition of irrigation water amounts to some six-hundred-billion gallons.

The Snowy Mountains Scheme was a significant employer of continental European migrants who endured the hardships and dangers of constructing these tunnels, dams, and powerhouses and contributed to the development of their new country.

Most fruit produced in Australia is raised on irrigated fields. Here, irrigated oranges are being harvested near Renmark by the Murray River in South Australia.

artesian aquifers, and enhancing soil productivity with fertilizers. Most parts of the environment have been subjected to shabby mistreatment, including such environmental treasures as the Great Barrier Reef and delicate rainforests. On a broader scale, the practice of *ringbarking* — girdling the bark of a tree so that it dies and allows more grass for livestock forage — is surprisingly widespread in a land of few trees. More incomprehensible, perhaps, is the massive overgrazing that is characteristic of most pastoral areas. Animal husbandry is the dominant rural activity of the nation, yet millions of acres have been denuded and subsequently eroded because of overstocking with sheep and cattle. Graziers often are quick to blame drought, kangaroos, or rabbits for the problem, but objective studies have shown that the critical factor usually is overgrazing by livestock.

Within the last two decades, a conservation consciousness of considerable breadth has arisen. Scattered adherents of the conservation crusade — *greenies* in the Aussie idiom — finally came together in 1983 to stop the damming of a wild river, the Gordon, in southwestern Tasmania. This was the first greenie victory in the conservation-versus-development arena, and signaled the coming of age of the conservation movement in Australia. Beginning with a few dedicated individuals and expanding into organized groups, the citizenry has led the government into more systematic and thoughtful consideration of resources, environment, and ecology.

PERSISTING PATTERNS

OF COLONIAL SETTLEMENT

The vast Australian land mass was far removed from the source regions of colonial immigrants. Both the size and remoteness of Australia, however, are critical to any understanding of the movement of non-Aboriginal peoples to and within Australia.

It was not until early in the seventeenth century that Australia was discovered by Europeans, and not until 1788 that the first European settlers arrived in Australia. The personnel of this "First Fleet" consisted mostly of convicts being deported from the overcrowded prisons of England to serve their sentences in this newly-established, distant penal colony. The site of the first settlement was only a stone's throw from the present heart of modern Sydney.

Several other penal settlements were established, all at coastal locations some distance removed from Sydney. British convicts continued to be exported to Australia for eight decades, in total numbering about 160,000. When the convicts had served out their sentences, some returned to Britain but most remained as "ticket-of-leave" free settlers in Australia. Mean-

The First Fleet — eleven ships containing nearly eight hundred convicts — arriving in Sydney Harbour early in 1788.

while, ordinary non-convict immigrants were increasingly attracted by the allure of a new land. By the 1830s free migrants outnumbered convicts, soon by a wide margin.

Six separate colonies were established at the time of early European settlement, a situation of fundamental importance in understanding the contemporary geography of Australia. These colonies developed separately, but similarly, throughout the nineteenth century. Thus, each of the six established its own administrative center or capital, principal port, and road and railway system that focused on the capital.

The pattern of settlement expansion was basically similar in each of the six colonies. From the initial coastal nuclei, explorers moved inland, primarily in a practical search for better farming or grazing land. Settlers followed hard on the heels of the explorers, who discovered only limited areas of potentially productive crop land but vast amounts of promising pastoral country. Thus there was a concentric spread inward from the coastal towns, with settlement denser nearer the coast (usually reflecting higher rainfall totals) and becoming sparser farther inland.

It became clear fairly early that livestock raising held more promise than crop growing, so most attention was focused on pastoralism. Several varieties of livestock were imported, but Merino sheep turned out to be far and away the most suitable. Emphasis on breeding and raising sheep for wool production changed the entire course of development of the first colony, New South Wales, and sheep raising became the economic lifeblood of the continent for many decades to come.

During the second half of the nineteenth century, settlement expanded to the furthest reaches of non-desert Australia and began to intensify. The colonial governments had made large grants of land to enterprising early settlers, and many of these holdings had been joined. Later settlers often "squatted" illegally on the land, and there were many years of problems with land alienation, land ownership, and land reform, the final result being an increase in the number of settlers and a decrease in the average size of the holdings.

THE AMERICAN GEOGRAPHICAL SOCIETY

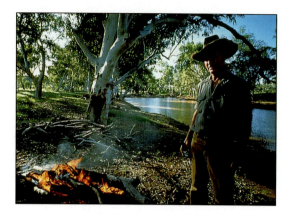

Independent ruggedness geared toward occupying the dry interior grasslands and woodlands has characterized much of Australia's history since European settlement began.

The six Australian colonies finally agreed to unite, and federation was achieved in 1901. At that time, the total population of the new country was less than two million people. The settlement pattern, however, was well developed; additions during the twentieth century have been mostly to intensify the colonial settlement pattern rather than to expand into new areas.

Distances are vast, population is scanty, and most activities are focused in a few widely scattered cities. Thus long distance transportation and communication networks are essential for the nation to function. The federal and state governments have taken a leading role in developing transportation, for the costs usually have been too great to attract much private development. A significant portion of each government's budget is for transportation, and nearly one-tenth of the Australian work force is employed in transportation, communications, and storage.

A sparse population scattered over a vast land area calls for an extensive network of roads but does not provide adequate financial support for the system. Thus, Australia has more than half a million miles of roadway, but fewer than twenty percent of the rural roads are paved and more than one-third of the mileage is sporadically maintained. Even so, the roadway network in the settled parts of the southeast is fairly complete and is heavily used. Australia boasts the third highest per capita vehicle ownership of any nation, with some six million licensed cars, trucks, and buses. Most of the traffic is in and around the cities, and traffic jams are a way of life for metropolitan Aussies. Roadway transport moves more than three-fourths of all domestic freight, but accounts for less than half of all ton-miles hauled.

Significant railway systems were built in each of the six Australian colonies during the latter half of the nineteenth century. In each colony the railroad net centered on the port-capital and was totally uncoordinated with the net in adjacent colonies. Even today, only ten interstate border crossings are made by rail lines.

The contemporary railway pattern of Australia is not well integrated. There are four state-owned systems— these in New South Wales, Victoria, Queensland, and Western Australia. A federal system operates the transcontinental line as well as virtually all the routes in South Australia, Tasmania, and the Northern Territory. Two specialized commuter networks are located in Melbourne and Adelaide. Half a dozen privately-owned, ore-carrying companies serve mining interests. The picture is further complicated by another colonial legacy — the fact that the railway systems in different states use different gauges, or track widths.

The role of railroads in Australia today is much the same as it was in the past, except that their relative importance has declined. Their principal function is still to funnel the primary products of a state to or through the capital city. As in most countries, the railways are best fitted for moving large loads on long hauls. The principal commodities carried are coal, other minerals, and agricultural produce. There is considerable competition with trucking lines for freight and with airlines for passengers.

Australians travel more miles by air, per capita, than do people of any other country. This is a fairly straightforward result of widely separated cities, a high standard of living, and good flying weather. Contemporary Australian commercial aviation is organized at four levels. Qantas is the government-owned airline and principal international carrier. Two domestic carriers, one of which is government owned, provide nationwide service. About a dozen smaller companies, most of them subsidiaries of the national carriers,

The Railway Gauge Problem

In the middle of the nineteenth century the six young Australian colonies were wrestling with the problem of starting railway systems. Among the many decisions to be made was choosing the width of gauge. As a general consideration, a narrower gauge results in less speed and less volume of traffic, but is also much less expensive to construct and equip. As the six colonies were separate, each would make and implement its own decision. However, the New South Wales and Victoria decisions were watched with interest by the other four since these were the most populous and prosperous colonies.

Great Britain had decided on the "standard" gauge of 4 feet 8.5 inches for its railways in the 1840s, and the Colonial Secretary recommended this gauge to the Australian colonies. However, the Chief Engineer of the Railways of New South Wales was an Irishman, and he insisted on using wide gauge, 5 feet 3 inches, perhaps because the Irish railways used that width. Accordingly, New South Wales adopted wide gauge in 1852, prior to the beginning of construction. This information was communicated to the other colonies, with the result that Victoria and South Australia also decided upon wide gauge.

However, the following year New South Wales appointed a different Chief Engineer, this time an Englishman, who arranged for the original plans to be changed in favor of standard gauge. It was some time before this change became known in the other colonies, and both Victoria and South Australia decided that it was too late to alter their designs, so they went ahead with wide gauge.

The other colonies — Queensland, Western Australia, and Tasmania — adopted narrow gauge, 3 feet 6 inches, because of its economy of cost. South Australia also initiated narrow gauge in the northern, sparsely-populated portion of the colony.

Thus the stage was set for impossible coordination among the railway systems of the various colonies. No two adjacent colonies had the same gauge except Victoria and part of South Australia. When the colonies federated in 1901 and became states, there began a lengthy series of discussions concerning gauge standardization, but action was very slow. Not until 1962 was there a common gauge (standard) on the railway line connecting Australia's two largest cities, Sydney and Melbourne. Since then the transcontinental line from Sydney to Perth has also been standardized, but almost everywhere else the colonial legacy of diverse railway gauges persists.

essentially operate as intrastate feeder lines. Another dozen still smaller companies function mostly at a regional level. In general, Australian civil aviation is efficient, heavily used, and characterized by a remarkable safety record.

Overseas connections by air and sea are numerous and important to the nation's economy. International sales absorb most of the output from the bellwether rural industries — mining, pastoralism, and farming. The flow of imports — especially petroleum, machinery, motor vehicles, chemicals, and textiles — to Australia is also important. Thus oceanic transport is a vital and booming activity at several dozen Australian ports. International air travel is also notable, with increasing numbers of both tourists and business travelers funneling through the major terminals of Sydney, Melbourne, Perth, and Brisbane.

Without doubt, however, it is movement within urban areas that is most notable in Australia. The vast majority of the people are urbanites and the economy is urban-centered. Thus daily commuter flows for employment, shopping trips, business, and recreational activities make the cities a beehive of traffic and pedestrian movement. Australian cities have a better mix of intraurban public transport (rail, bus, and trolley) than most US cities, but notably less developed freeway systems.

Perth, capital of Western Australia and one of Australia's fastest growing cities, exemplifies the dynamic urban nature of Australian society.

THE AMERICAN GEOGRAPHICAL SOCIETY

THE REGIONAL MOSAIC

Although Australia has less physical and cultural variety than any other of the settled continents, there are, nonetheless, regional differences. The continent can be divided into six major regions — Southeastern Fringe, Mediterranean Corners, Tasmania, Northeastern Fringe, Monsoonal North, and The Dry Lands — each of which will be discussed briefly below.

The "heartland" of Australia — the Southeastern Fringe — consists of a crescent of land that extends southward from northern New South Wales

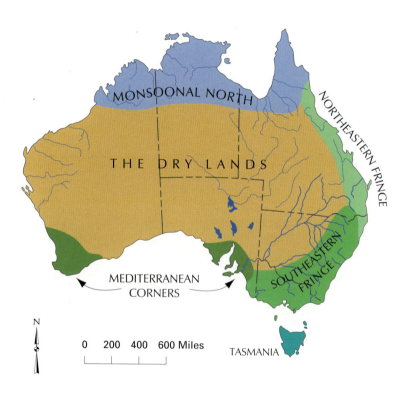

The major regions of Australia.

The Tweed River, near Murwillumbah, New South Wales, with Mount Warning in the background — a scene in the Southeastern Fringe.

along the eastern coastal fringe of the continent into the southeastern corner of South Australia. This region contains the largest cities, the busiest ports, the most heavily used roads and railways, the principal industrial areas, most of the densely settled agricultural and pastoral districts, many coastal resorts, and major coal mining areas. It is by no means uniformly an area of dense settlement and bustling activities, however. Large areas of rugged hill country and dense forest are included. Indeed, some of Australia's most impenetrable wildernesses are scattered through this coastal zone.

A generalized land use model of the region would show a discontinuous series of small coastal lowlands and river valleys occupied by fairly intensive farming and pastoral enterprises and a number of variously-sized urban centers. These lowlands are backed by short but steep slopes leading into hill and low mountain lands that are partly covered with dense eucalyptus forests and partly grassed. These latter areas are devoted to grazing of sheep, cattle, and goats. Inland from the hill country is an expansive farming zone where sheep and grains are grown on properties of moderate size. This general pattern is interrupted in various places by irrigated districts of diversified farm output, and the entire region is dominated by the major metropolises of Sydney and Melbourne.

This region contains some sixty percent of Australia's population. The concentration of people here is partly because of historical and political factors, but is mostly due to the more favorable environmental conditions, particularly the quantity and dependability of rainfall. Easterly winds, responses to summer low pressure in the interior, bring Pacific moisture onshore. This moist airstream is forced up the slopes of the Eastern Highlands, which produces widespread precipitation. In winter the region is dominated by westerly air flow that brings with it variable air masses, fronts, and storms. This is the only part of Australia, except Tasmania, that receives relatively reliable precipitation year-round. This reliable rainfall provides the basic necessity for dependable growing of crops and pastures.

Mineral resources in the region are limited, except for supplies of the major hydrocarbons — coal, petroleum, and natural gas. The extensive deposits of bituminous coal that reach the surface about one hundred miles north, south, and west of Sydney fostered the devel-

The Federal Parliament building in Canberra, Australian Capital Territory. Canberra is Australia's capital and largest inland city.

opment of iron and steel industries at Newcastle and Wollongong, two of Australia's three largest non-capital cities. In the Latrobe Valley, east of Melbourne, is the world's largest continuous deposit of lignite coal; it is used to generate most of the electricity for the state of Victoria. Australia's most important areas of petroleum and natural gas production are beneath the waters of Bass Strait off the coast of eastern Victoria.

The region, and the nation, are dominated by the two metropolises of the coastal lowlands. Sydney and Melbourne combined contain nearly forty percent of the country's population; some 3.6 million in the former and 3.2 million in the latter. Although the sites of the two cities are quite different, their locational advantages and historical development are remarkably similar. Today each of the cities ranks either first or second in virtually every conceivable urban superlative of Australia.

The Southeastern Fringe also contains Canberra, a completely planned city that is the national capital and the nation's largest inland city.

Australia has two Mediterranean "Corners" — areas of Mediterranean climate notable in that winter is the rainy season and summer is virtually rainless. One of these areas focuses on Adelaide in South Australia and the other in the vicinity of Perth in Western Australia. These two areas are separated by the broad indentation of the Great Australian Bight, along whose coast the waters of the Southern Ocean meet the desert of interior Australia.

Most of the world's Mediterranean lands have a natural vegetation cover that is dominated by shrubs. In Australia's Mediterranean Corners, however, forests and woodlands are extensive, presumably because many species of eucalyptus are quite drought resistant and thus able to cope with rainless summers. Forests are particularly notable south of Perth, where the wetter areas contain extensive tracts of tall *karri* trees which can grow to heights exceeding three hundred feet. The less humid zone has even more expansive forests of *jarrah*, which can reach one-hundred-fifty feet in height. In the vicinity of Adelaide the forests and woodlands are considerably less vast, and the trees are less useful economically.

Dairying and mixed farming are common around both Perth and Adelaide, but the distinctive agriculture of this region consists of irrigated specialty crops, such as orchards, vineyards, and

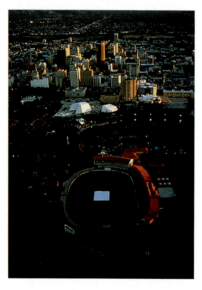

Looking south across the Oval to the heart of Adelaide, beyond which is the famous greenbelt and, in the distance, the Mount Lofty ranges.

market gardens. Australia's most famous wine area is the Barossa Valley, some thirty miles north of Adelaide, but there are several other outstanding vineyard areas. Both citrus and deciduous fruits are also widely grown; particularly notable are oranges along the lower Murray River and apples in several valleys about one hundred miles south of Perth.

Despite large areas of forest and notable concentrations of specialized agriculture, most of the area of the Mediterranean region is devoted to growing

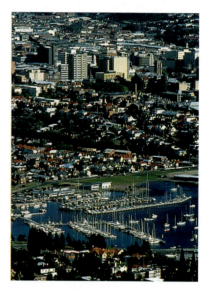

Hobart, capital of Tasmania, is a market center and the state's chief port. The annual Sydney to Hobart yacht race ends here.

grains or raising sheep or to the typical wheat/sheep operation that is widespread in southeastern Australia. Monocultural grain farms are more widespread in this region than anywhere else in the nation. Wheat is normally the dominant crop, except in parts of the mallee country and on the Eyre Peninsula, where barley is the leader. As wheat and barley are both winter grains, the lack of summer rain is no handicap to their production.

These Mediterranean portions of Australia contain more than ninety percent of the people of their respective states, and contain the only significant population concentrations not located close to the eastern or southeastern coasts. Adelaide and Perth are the capitals, chief ports, and dominant commercial, financial, and industrial centers of their states. Although different in terms of site and history, there is much similarity between the two cities.

The island of Tasmania is large, but the state is small by Australian standards and encompasses less than one percent of the nation's area. Its population is also small — a bit less than 500,000 — but abundant rainfall provides conditions that have allowed a relatively high density of population, second only to Victoria among the states.

Tasmania's mid-latitude location distinguishes it from the rest of the country in terms of climate (colder winters, more dependable precipitation), natural vegetation (more trees in general and more and denser forests in particular), and water resources (an abundance of permanent streams). Moreover, Tasmania's terrain is almost entirely slopeland, varying from gentle to exceedingly rugged.

Agricultural development has been limited by a lack of flat land and productive soils. Where favorable conditions prevail, however, there is mixed farming on a more intensive scale than is usual on the mainland. Farmers tend to specialize in relatively high value crops — such as apples, hops, berries, and potatoes — so that the quantity of output and its dollar value are well above the Australian average. Livestock are also prominent in the farm scene: sheep, primarily raised for meat, and beef cattle are widespread, but dairying is more typical.

Tasmania has a much lower concentration of metropolitan population than any other state. Only about one-third of the population lives in Hobart, and the second city, Launceston, is nearly half as large as the capital, a pattern unprecedented in other Australian states. The remainder of the population is spread fairly evenly over the agricultural districts, with a number of small cities along the north coast.

Most of the northern and central portions of Australia's east coast are included within the Northeastern Fringe, a region that has a warm, wet climate. This subtropical environment favors the growth of a number of plants that are either absent or rare in the rest of the continent. Prior to the arrival of Europeans, this coastal stretch contained many disconnected patches of tropical rainforest, which is unlike any other plant community in Australia. With the arrival of European settlers, tropical and subtropical crops — most notably sugar cane, bananas, and pineapple — were introduced, adding another distinctive note to both the landscape and the economy. Offshore is the Great Barrier Reef, yet another unique aspect of the region.

European settlers came into the Northeastern Fringe from the south. A branch penal colony was established in 1825 where Brisbane now stands, but it only lasted fifteen years. Early pastoralists worked their way northward on the inland side of the mountain ranges, and used the river valleys to reach the coast. Other settlers moved more slowly northward along the coast, in search of arable farmland. Gold rushes in interior Queensland, particularly in the 1860s, quickened the pace of settlement as disappointed prospectors and miners turned to farming.

All sugar cane is now harvested mechanically, as on this farm near Mossman in northern Queensland.

Sugar cane became the distinctive crop of the region, and was produced up and down the coast for twelve hundred miles, from Coffs Harbour in the south to Mossman in the north. Sugar production leapfrogged from one coastal valley to the next in search of the right combination of soil, warmth, and moisture. There are now some eight thousand cane growers in the region, with farms that average about seventy acres in size.

Despite the prominence of specialized tropical crops, dairying is actually more widespread in these coastal areas. Nearly one-third of Australia's dairy cattle are kept here. In the drier coastal stretches and on the inland side of the region crop farming is rare, and most of the land is either in forest or used for grazing livestock. This is a part of Australia where sheep proved unsuitable, and cattle breeding and fattening are the principal livestock activities.

Prominent rural industries notwithstanding, this coastal region is primarily famous for its subtropical coastal resorts and the wonders of the Great Barrier Reef. It is the premier tourist

World-class surfing is one of the many water sports available in Australia.

destination for urban Australians and is second only to Sydney as a goal of international visitors.

Some 2.4 million people, about one-seventh of Australia's population, reside in this region. The distribution of the rural portion of this population is a direct reflection of the land use pattern — forest areas are unpopulated, beef cattle districts are sparsely settled, and areas of more intensive land use (sugar, dairying, etc.) have moderately high densities. Growing towns and ports have evolved to serve the region. Greater Brisbane contains about forty-five percent of the regional population, and there are other significant cities along the coast, with Gold Coast (250,000) in the south and Townsville (100,000) in the north being the two largest.

The Monsoonal North — roughly the northernmost twenty percent of the continent — can be identified as a region that is distinctive in character because of the dominance of a monsoonal climate — warm, rainy summers and long, mild, dry winters. This is a sparsely populated region of extensive beef cattle raising and widespread Aboriginal occupancy.

The natural vegetation that has evolved under this specialized climate is largely a grassy woodland. The tree cover consists mostly of various species of eucalyptus growing in an open pattern, although there are a few patches of dense forest, even rainforest. Almost everywhere a prominent grassy understory spreads beneath the trees.

The majority of the region consists of extensive flattish plains, seamed by many rivers that are raging torrents in summer but are often reduced to trickles or total dryness in winter. There are extensive rugged rocky hills in the Kimberleys District of Western Australia and a prominent, scarp-edged sandstone plateau in Arnhem Land.

The only abiding activity that has supported rural settlement by whites in this region is extensive cattle raising, and that has sustained only a very

Darwin, rebuilt after devastation by Cyclone Tracy in 1974, is the administrative and commercial hub of the Northern Territory.

sparse population. Otherwise, the economic output of the region is limited to a handful of farms, a few large mines, and some specialized fisheries.

The Monsoonal North is one of the few parts of Australia where Aborigines comprise a sizable proportion of the population. Many of them are fringe dwellers in the towns, undereducated, underemployed, occupying the lowest rungs of the socio-economic ladder, and depending largely on government welfare payments for their livelihood. Others occupy traditional tribal areas, maintaining some tribal cohesion and cultural identity, circumstances most notable in Arnhem Land. Within the last decade the federal government has enacted legislation that pertains only to the Northern Territory whereby Aborigines may gain title, via collective Land Trusts and Land Councils, to "traditional" lands. Through this mechanism about one-third of the area of the Northern Territory portion of the Monsoonal North region has come under Aboriginal control.

The only urban place of any size in this region is the administrative center of the Northern Territory, Darwin. Although long established, Darwin has never had a viable economy and has depended upon heavy infusions of government spending. It now has a population exceeding seventy thousand and is one of the fastest-growing cities in the country, although government spending and tourism are almost the only economic supports.

Australia's largest, most remote, and least densely occupied region is a vast arid and semiarid expanse here called The Dry Lands. This region includes almost two-thirds of the area of the continent, but contains only about six percent of the continental population. It is too dry for farming without irrigation, too remote from water sources for irrigation, and too barren for animal husbandry other than extensive grazing. Thus human occupancy is restricted mostly to widely dispersed pastoral homesteads, scattered Aboriginal settlements, several important mining centers, and a limited number of small towns.

The central theme of the regional climate is the dominance of both perennial and episodic drought. For most of the region, drought is continuous

> ## Aboriginal Desert Dwellers
>
> The earliest Australians came via land and sea when sea level was lower during the last Ice Age and settled on the Australian mainland and on the Torres Strait Islands.
>
> When Europeans arrived they found these hunter-gatherers living in family groups and often moving from place to place in a seasonal pattern between encampments. Estimates of their total numbers range from between three-hundred thousand to one million. These peoples spoke two hundred separate languages. They were called "Aboriginal" because to European eyes they were primitive — they had little in the way of clothing, material possessions, tools, or technology. Europeans believed that technology indicated intelligence, so the Aborigines were seen as stupid — pre-human, animal-like; and they were treated accordingly. Their population declined disastrously until the 1950s, at which time government policy became more humane.
>
> A closer look at the Aboriginal way of life, however, reveals a culture rich beyond its sparse material trappings. The Aborigines were delicately in tune with their land, and perceived an abundance of resources. For an Aboriginal resident of Australia's Western Desert, the land was rich in animal and plant life. With their tracking abilities and detailed knowledge of the environment, these earliest residents gathered the food and water needed for sustenance. They used spears, boomerangs, digging sticks, and dishes — easy to carry, easy to replace.
>
> The Aborigines sometimes had time left over from providing the necessities of life to spend on religion, art, ceremony, and intricate interactions within their family groups. They saw their Western Desert as a beloved home, a friendly, secure place, as long as they lived according to the law established by their gods.

and is interrupted only by brief intervals of sporadic rainfall. The northern margin receives about twenty-two inches of rainfall annually, but most areas receive less than half that amount. Rainfall is not only scarce but also unreliable, and great variations from the norm can be expected in any given year. The clear skies and direct sunlight of summer produce very high temperatures; readings in excess of 100°F can be expected for many weeks. Night temperatures are considerably lower because the heat is quickly lost in the clear atmosphere. Winter days are usually warm to hot, but nights cool significantly, with most parts of the region having below-freezing temperatures at night, at least occasionally.

This is the classic land of the Ab-

> They believed that their part-animal, part-human ancestors built the hills, creek-beds, and waterholes of the Australian landscape during the ancient creation period known as the "Dreamtime."
>
> To preserve and protect native culture, the Australian Institute of Aboriginal Studies was established in 1964. It has promoted Aboriginal and Torres Strait Islander studies in the arts, education, language, health, history, and other areas. In 1984, with amendments in succeeding years, a law was passed that protects places, areas, and objects of particular significance to Aboriginal tradition. This law buttressed the power of the Aboriginal Land Rights (Northern Territory) Act of 1976, which gave land title of about one-third of the Northern Territory to native groups. Since the 1970s, tracts of land in other states have also been deeded back to their original inhabitants.
>
> Many of Australia's most famous landscapes are in national parks on Aboriginal reserve lands, and these are co-managed by Aboriginal Councils and the Australian National Parks and Wildlife Service. Ayers Rock in Uluru National Park is one of these places, sacred to the Aborigine and to many other humans worldwide. Other parks under this style of management include Kakadu, Nitmiluk, and Gurig national parks.
>
> Aboriginal arts — dance, music, painting, traditional crafts, graphic design, and story-telling — are also undergoing a rebirth. As this native population becomes part of mainstream modern-day Australia, its ancient way of life is also reviving, respected as it was once despised, being nourished back from the edge of extinction to assume a place of valued significance in contemporary Australian society.

origine. Aboriginal people occupied every part of the continent prior to the coming of Europeans, but they were soon displaced from or inundated by whites in the more favored areas. The harsh environment of the Outback was less attractive to the whites and offered fewer opportunities for them, so the Aborigines here were less pressured and have maintained a significant presence in the region.

Well over half of the total Aboriginal population of Australia is found in this region. They live in a variety of situations: some are town fringe-dwellers, some are wage-earners on cattle stations, increasing numbers (but still a small proportion) are employed at mines or other enterprises, and most are concentrated in distinctive Ab-

THE AMERICAN GEOGRAPHICAL SOCIETY

A young Aborigine prepares another for a traditional dance.

original settlements. Some of these settlements were founded and/or maintained as church missions for paternalistic ministering to Aboriginals. Most were set up by the government as Aboriginal "reserves" similar to Indian reservations in the United States. Others have been established by the Aboriginals themselves, often with significant government funding, to serve as focal points for Aboriginal concentrations in a white society. Schooling and social services are generally available in these settlements, but gainful employment is scarce.

Apart from the Aboriginal presence mentioned above, most settlements in the region are pastoral stations, and by far the most pervasive land use is the extensive grazing of livestock. With the notable exception of some areas in Western Australia, there is a clear-cut separation of wool and beef operations. A pastoralist raises either sheep or cattle, but not both. Merino sheep dominate on the eastern and western margins of the region; it is no coincidence that these are the better-watered and better-grassed portions. Beef cattle are found elsewhere.

Various other schemes have been devised to "develop" some portion of the region, but, with limited exceptions, only mining has been successful

THE AMERICAN GEOGRAPHICAL SOCIETY

Aboriginal art has gained significant momentum and widespread appreciation in recent years.

in this endeavor.

The lure of the desert is finally being exploited as a tourist attraction that entices more and more short-term visitors to the region. Alice Springs, situated almost exactly in the center of the continent, is the hub of this activity, with new hotels, golf courses, and even a gambling casino in this unlikely spot. Three hundred miles to the southwest by a newly-paved highway is Uluru National Park, which contains Ayers Rock. The twin allure of "The Alice" and "The Rock" bring several hundred thousand visitors to the center of the continent each year.

AROUND THE WORLD PROGRAM **AUSTRALIA**

THE AMERICAN GEOGRAPHICAL SOCIETY

THE GOOD LUCK

WILL IT CONTINUE?

The area of Australia is almost exactly the same as that of the forty-eight conterminous United States, but its population is only one-fifteenth as large. Despite major differences in the environments of the two countries, Australia is fairly easy to comprehend for an American because the common Anglo-Saxon background has produced a multitude of cultural, social, political, and economic similarities. The American will soon note certain "peculiarities" in Aussie society — a parliamentary political system, voting requirements that are both mandatory and preferential, a relatively high degree of government regulation of many aspects of everyday life, a very powerful

Australia and the United States are almost equal in area.

AUSTRALIA AROUND THE WORLD PROGRAM

and militant complex of labor unions, a much more restrictive land tenure system, etc. — but for the most part a "Yank" experiences little in the way of culture shock Down Under.

Australia often has been referred to as the "lucky country." Lucky to have been established by Britain when Britain was a benevolently successful colonial power. Lucky because it has been spared much of the tension and trouble that beset other parts of the world. Lucky because it has resources in abundance to support its development. Lucky because it was remote from the seats of competing powers and therefore not a region to be fought over. Lucky because its Aboriginal inhabitants were few, unsophisticated, peaceful, and easily displaced. Lucky because its contemporary population is relatively homogeneous and cohesive. Lucky because it never experienced revolution or war on its home territory. Lucky because it has never had to contend with population pressures.

In international relations, Australia's world view has been necessarily fashioned by geographical isolation. Located half a world away from the mother country and alienated by culture and custom from nearby Asian neighbors, Australians have generally and understandably been much more concerned with domestic affairs than they have with international events. The principal exception for many decades was the country's close liaison with Great Britain, which was the colonizing homeland, the source of most imports, the purchaser of most exports, and the paternalistic guide in foreign affairs. However, as a result of World War II and Britain's eventual joining of the European Economic Community, this relationship withered. The importance of alliance with the United States became undeniable, although not as dogmatically as had previously been the case with Britain.

More recently Australia has fostered increasing ties with various Asian nations, a practical recognition of certain mutual interests with countries that are geographical neighbors. In essence, Australia is striving to assume a comfortable stance as a "semi-Asian" country, as demonstrated by actual and potential trade relationships and a broadened immigration policy.

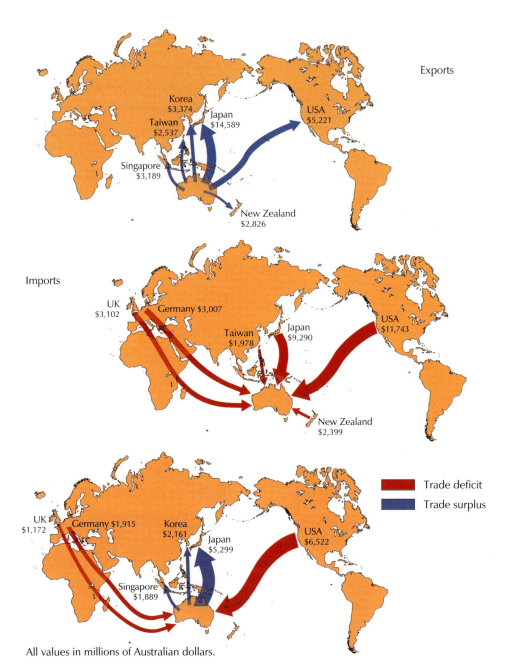

Australia's exports (top), imports (middle), and balance of international trade (bottom) in 1991–1992.

What can be predicted about Australia's future? By any objective standard, it is still the lucky country. It still has remarkable quantities of natural resources, and the potential of others being discovered is great; it has been spared the threat and problems of overpopulation; and it has been able to maintain a generally high standard of living by finding markets for its products.

But such good fortune cannot be taken for granted. It is all too easy for a boom to turn into a boomerang. It is not enough to be a relatively underpopulated, relatively unpolluted storehouse of riches for the world. Despite its great potential, its recent economic growth per capita has been slower than that of almost any "developed" nation. Enterprise and innovation and initiative seem to have been blunted by the lure of a leisurely and comfortable way of life, by an inward-looking insularity that favors protection over production. Economic and social problems are becoming more common. In comparison with most of the rest of the world, the Aussies have a good life — but not as good as it used to be.

The Coat of Arms of the Commonwealth of Australia.
Permission to reproduce the Arms granted by the Australian Government Department of Administrative Services.

Geographical Milestones
in Australian History

≥40,000 BC	Ancestors of Aborigines arrived in Australia.
AD 1606	Willem Jansz became first European to sight and land on Australia.
1770	James Cook explored Australia's east coast, claimed the land for Great Britain, and named it New South Wales.
1788	"First Fleet" of settlers, mostly convicts, landed at Botany Bay, and soon transferred to Port Jackson Bay.
1792	First non-convict immigrants arrived from Great Britain.
1801–1803	Matthew Flinders sailed completely around Australia, proving it to be one land mass.
1805	First extensive sheep-raising enterprise began.
1851	Major gold deposits discovered in New South Wales and Victoria.
1861	World's first freezing works built in Sydney; led to meat exports.
1868	Great Britain ended transportation of convicts to Australia.
1901	Six British colonies united to form independent nation of Australia, with Melbourne as temporary capital; constitution accepted.
1914–1918	60,000 Australians died in World War; increased sense of nationalism.
1920	Air transportation began in Australia.
1927	Canberra became new federal capital; located in Australian Capital Territory.
1939–1945	Australia engaged in World War; United States forces in Pacific based in Australia 1942–1943.
1951	ANZUS Treaty signed by Australia, New Zealand, and the United States; this was first effort to formalize relations between Australia and the United States.
1966	Immigration policy revised; significant restrictions removed formally in response to increasingly liberal immigration policy.
1967	Australian Constitution amended to permit federal programs to aid Aborigines.
1975	Papua-New Guinea became independent of Australia; agreement on boundary reached in 1978.
1994	South Pacific Forum, including Australia and fourteen other nations, agreed to interact cooperatively to manage regional resources.

Sources of
ADDITIONAL INFORMATION

LITERATURE

Atlas of Australian Resources. Various dates. Canberra: Division of National Mapping.

Australian Encyclopedia. 1985. Boston: G. K. Hall & Co.

Blainey, G. 1975. *Triumph of the Nomads: A History of Ancient Australia.* Melbourne: Macmillan Company of Australia.

Clark, C. M. H. 1962–1978. *A History of Australia.* Melbourne: Melbourne University Press, four volumes.

Harrell, M. A. 1989. *Surprising Lands Down Under.* Washington: National Geographic Society.

Jeans, D. N. (editor). 1986–1987. *Australia: A Geography.* Sydney: Sydney University Press, second edition, two volumes.

Learmonth, N., and A. Learmonth. 1971. *Regional Landscapes of Australia: Form, Function, Change.* Sydney: Angus Press.

McKnight, T. L. 1995. *Oceania: The Geography of Australia, New Zealand, and the Pacific Islands.* Englewood Cliffs, NJ: Prentice Hall.

Powell, J. M. 1988. *An Historical Geography of Modern Australia: The Restive Fringe.* New York: Cambridge University Press.

Terrill, R. 1987. *The Australians.* New York: Simon and Schuster.

IMPORTANT ADDRESSES

Australian Tourist Commission
   2121 Avenue of the Stars, Suite 1200
   Los Angeles, California 90067
   Telephone: 310-552-1988

Embassy of Australia
   1601 Massachusetts Avenue, NW
   Washington, DC 20036-2273
   Telephone: 202-797-3000

AUSTRALIA
at a Glance

Official Name	Commonwealth of Australia
Derivation of the Name	"Southern," from the Latin *australis*
Short Name	Australia
Official Flag	Blue field with red, white, and blue British Union Jack in upper left, five white stars representing Southern Cross constellation on right, and one large white star representing the country's states and territories in lower left
Anthems	*Advance Australia Fair* (national); *God Save the Queen* (royal)
Term for Citizens	Australian; "Aussie"
Form of government	Federal Parliament
Area	2,965,868 square miles
Population	16,930,000 (1991 census); 17,600,000 estimated 1995
Percent Urban	86
Official Language	English
National Capital	Canberra
Most Populous City	Sydney (3,600,000 in 1995)
Currency	Dollar (plural: dollars) (approximately 1.26 dollars AUS = 1 dollar US in 1996)
Mean Annual Income	Per capita GNP = $19,300 (1995)
Prominent Ethnic Groups	British, Italian, German, Greek, Dutch
Dominant Religions	Anglican (ca. 33%); Roman Catholic (ca. 25%); Uniting Church of Australia (ca. 20%)
Major National Holidays	January 1 (New Year's Day), January 26 (Australia Day), (Easter), April 25 (Anzac Day), first or second Monday in June (Queen's Birthday), December 25 (Christmas)
National Sports	Horse racing, cricket, Aussie rules football, rugby league, rugby union, soccer, swimming, surfing, tennis, golf, basketball, two-up